THE
BLUFFER'S GUIDE
TO
MARKETING

GRAHAM HARDING
& PAUL WALTON

Oval Books

Published by Oval Books
335 Kennington Road
London SE11 4QE
United Kingdom

Telephone: +44 (0)20 7582 7123
Fax: +44 (0)20 7582 1022
E-mail: info@ovalbooks.com

First published by Ravette Publishing, 1987
Reprinted/updated: 1989,1991,1992,1993,
1995,1996,1997,1998

First published by Oval Books, 1999
Updated 2000, 2003

Series Editor – Anne Tauté

Cover designer – Jim Wire, Quantum
Printer – Cox & Wyman Ltd
Producer – Oval Projects Ltd

The Bluffer's Guides® series is based
on an original idea by Peter Wolfe.

The Bluffer's Guide®, The Bluffer's
Guides®, Bluffer's®, and Bluff Your
Way® are Registered Trademarks.

ISBN: 1-902825-94-2

CONTENTS

Jargon:

Diagrams:

THE MARKETING CONCEPT

Marketing activity involves taking something simple and obvious and packaging it to go. This is a skill which all good bluffers quickly learn.

The idea of marketing itself is no exception. In lay terms the marketing concept means that you stand a better chance of flogging something if you understand whether and why someone wants it in the first place.

But to the marketing man and woman, **The Marketing Concept** is very serious stuff, as important as The Meaning of Life. In fact to many successful marketeers it *is* the meaning of life and the best bluffers will show a reverence towards it which echoes a lawyer's belief in the rule of law or a doctor's in the Hippocratic Oath.

The marketing concept is to be differentiated in business strategy from a number of other misguided and inferior approaches:

The Production Concept

Produce what we sell. This is an immensely inward-looking, technology-worshipping approach which can easily produce better mousetraps that nobody wants to buy.

The Sales Concept

Sell what we produce. This is a slightly more evolved view of business and accordingly is either staggeringly successful or absolutely catastrophic. Its ruling classes are the salesmen.

The Trading Concept

Buy a little, sell a little and make a little.

The Accountancy Concept

Forget the products, 'think numbers'. If it doesn't help the bottom line it's not worth doing. Increasingly in the ascendant.

As a well-read bluffer in marketing, you will recognise lower forms of business orientation and demonstrate the superiority of the marketing concept at every possible moment.

A good stratagem in meetings where people temporarily forget what marketing is about, is to trot out a suitably learned homily for reminding your audience about the magic of the marketing concept. A few maxims for marketeers include the following:

'Marketing is human activity directed at satisfying needs and wants through exchange processes'– P. Kotler. Boring, but sound.

'The job of the marketeer is to get the best fit between company resources and consumer needs' – Hugh Davidson. Good with non-marketing colleagues.

'Marketing is disciplined demand management.' Particularly useful when your marketing director is more interested in your advertising than he is in your volume forecasts.

'The purpose of marketing is to earn a profit by adding the maximum value at the minimum cost' – C. McIver. Very useful in agency negotiations when they submit some outlandish production invoice.

'Marketing is the intelligence service of the corporate army' – Anon.

Then there is the drinks party question: 'And what do *you* do?' More often than not, you will have to defend yourself against accusations of using all manner of techniques to persuade the consumer (i.e. everyone else in the room) to buy products they don't need by the use of expensive advertising that they have to pay for.

The argument that marketing is a humanistic philosophy, making the consumer the centre of the universe, will not wash with clever lawyers, superior accountants or left-wing intellectuals who can smell blood. The best bluffers will avoid any introduction of themselves containing the word marketing. Much safer gambits are:

- Business (mysterious – trading? the City?)
- Research (nicely ambiguous but avoid this one with academics in the room)
- General Management (sounds impressive)
- Industry (sound, but dull)
- Innovation (different, but hard to live up to)

The wise will resist the temptation to explain the ways of the marketing world to the masses. The media is only interest in marketing is making good television out of the marketeer's discomfort. You have been warned.

Marketing as Warfare

Unless you're a pacifist, treat marketing as war. It doesn't matter whether it's war against your colleagues, war against your suppliers, war against your channels of distribution or war against your competitors. War is a good metaphor for the business of marketing. You can discuss frontal assaults, pincer movements, guerrilla warfare. You can talk of shock troops, supply chains, tactical withdrawals, the chain of command.

Best of all for serious bluffers is the art of war – Japanese style. The classic text is Miyamoto Musashi's *A Book of Five Rings*. This 17th-century Teach Yourself Strategy for samurai contains all the budding international marketeer need know about making his or her way in the world. For example:

'In all forms of strategy it is necessary to maintain the combat stance in everyday life and to make your everyday stance your combat stance.'

'In strategy it is important to see distant things as if they were close and to take a distanced view of close things.'

'Suppress the enemy's useful actions but allow his useless actions.'

Whilst you are putting up this smokescreen you should not neglect the Home Front. Establish a reputation for inside information. Manoeuvre for position with your boss. Lastly, consider the assignments that will bring glory without unnecessary exposure to risk.

Marketing Neuroses

Marketing people are prone to several complexes and good bluffers will know about them. In certain cases they will be *affected* so as to look the part properly, in others *sublimated* to avoid being cast as villain of the piece or sacked. So care is needed in applying this knowledge.

Integration

What marketeers mean by 'integration' is that marketing has to be the top-gun in the boardroom. Not everyone shares this view.

As young marketing trainees discover – life is not pure Kotler and there are many companies where marketing is neither the centre of the universe nor the centre of the 'organisational wheel'. In fact there are many companies where the Chairman's wife or the motorcycle couriers are more 'integrated' than the marketing department.

The lessons for successful marketing bluffers are:

a) Understand the 'culture' of the company

This means who runs the company and who sets the house rules. It could be 'marketing' or a marketeer. It might just as well be:

> The Family
> The Chairman
> The Chairman's Mistress
> The Chairman's Hitman
> Sales
> Finance
> Production
> R & D
> The Typing Pool

In a sales dominated business, you should write their scripts, show lots of energy, be part of the 'solution', never 'part of the problem', show interest (but not too much) in their customers and have plenty of action plans. Don't waste your time trying to sell them marketing as the Harvard Business School teaches it, unless you are mentally deficient, a masochist or both.

b) **Acknowledge that what marketing is and what marketing people do are different things.**

As many marketeers demonstrate every day, you do not have to know what marketing is to work in the marketing department.

If you find yourself in a company where marketing is not central and where your boss thinks the Boston Matrix is a wrestling hold, do not despair. If it suits you, have fun enjoying the pleasant things that marketing people do, like awaydays and trips to the agency. If it doesn't suit you, spend your time constructively polishing your CV for eventual relaunch into a more heavy duty marketing situation.

At all costs do not be neurotic about integration unless the culture is.

Selling

Because marketing is currently in vogue, everybody is getting into it. In popular usage, marketing has come to mean selling with a college education, as in:

Marketing Area	Done by
Property	Estate agents, Timeshare sharks
Non Profit Sector	Theatres and galleries
Practice Development	Solicitors and accountants
Energy Conservation	Double Glazing companies
Financial Services	Life Insurance companies and banks
Educational Services	Renamed polytechnics
Personal Services	Cards in phone boxes

When you are confronted with someone who confuses your rôle with selling, the best strategy is to suggest that you are as much involved in selling as Shakespeare was in acting, or, if in the company of other marketeers, suggest that good marketing makes selling unnecessary.

Yet another stratagem is to agree wholeheartedly – "Yes, of course, I'm in the business of selling ideas". It's called repositioning yourself as a Communications Consultant.

The Diffusion of Marketing and The Marketing of Diffusion

Diffusion is what most marketing people believe happened to one-time cult objects such as Porsche and Filofax. (These days, red braces are out and worksteads and cocooning are in, says Faith Popcorn, lady of the thousand trends.)

What you have to do is get your product adopted by the trendsetters and spend such money you have on persuading them of its exclusivity. Then, so the idea runs, it will spread from its original niche in Covent Garden wine bars or Los Angeles racquet clubs to the lesser breeds of today's acquisitive society. And you will make money.

The successful bluffer will argue cogently that it's quite possible to diffuse too fast.

The other key thing to know about diffusion is that, technically speaking, it is the diffusion curve that is the important thing.

You will affect to be one of the early majority ('a man of the people') but you will wish others to see you as either an innovator or one of the early adopters

11

The Diffusion of Innovations

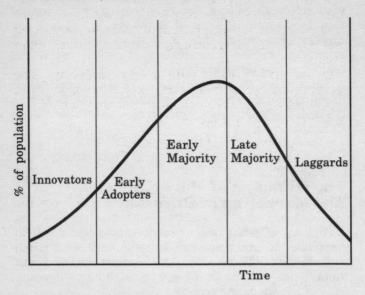

(the trend watchers), and will act accordingly. On no account should you be seen as one of the late majority or, God forbid, one of the laggards.

The great thing about diffusion from the bluffer's point of view is that *everything* (products, people, regions of the country, attitudes, illnesses, companies, even whole industries) can be skewered neatly on the curve. Take marketing itself for example:

The innovators were the American FMCG (see Glossary) companies who adopted marketing in the 1950s. Procter and Gamble were one of the first and are still one of the best of the 'blue-chip' marketing companies.

The early adopters – in the 1960s – included the drinks and beverages companies. They have stayed pretty good at it, but you might score by suggesting that they are increasingly reactive rather than 'proactive'.

In the 1970s came **the early majority**. The retailers discovered marketing; computer companies thought they had. For evidence that they hadn't you need only cite their inability to:

a) create any powerful brands, and
b) recognise user benefits rather than product benefits.

The late majority in the marketing ball were the financial services companies who came piling in, during the 1980s. You need only cite the indistinguishable TV advertising and the paucity of branding in insurance ads to prove the obvious clichés about them.

The laggards include politics and publishing, only now waking up to marketing. Following the American example, politicians have polished the image of their parties, thrown themselves headlong into direct mail and embraced the market research and positioning paraphernalia of marketing companies. Unkindly, one might say that the problem is the basic products.

Turning a problem into an opportunity (as all marketeers should) you will see that the route to power and success in marketing is to take the gospel to one of the laggards. Marketing is now given lip service in big financial institutions but there are still many businesses where a little marketing bluff will take you a long way.

SPEAKING THE LANGUAGE

Marketing has an extensive cloud of unknowing hanging over it. This takes the form of jargon. You deplore the over-use of jargon but this should not stop you using it for all you're worth.

Rule 1: Always refer to the market in which you operate in terms which are incomprehensible to any literate outsider:

Never	*Always*
Butter and margarine	— Yellow Fats
Radios, Televisions, etc.	— Brown Goods
Washing machines, fridges etc.	— White Goods
Spuds	— White Veg
Bars of chocolate	— Countlines
Knickers	— Intimate Apparel
Hot Meal Lubricant	— Gravy

Rule 2: Complicate rather than simplify:

Reasons for buying	— Composite Explanatory Variables
Idea / Good Idea	— Concept / Key concept
Bad idea	— Interesting concept
Disagree	— Play Devil's Advocate
Gradual	— Evolutionary
New	— Revolutionary
What we're going to do	— Strategy
Needs	— Need States
Intrinsics	— The Ingredients
Extrinsics	— The image/packaging

Rule 3: Turn the obvious questions on their heads. Do not ask "Is there a gap in the market?" Ask, as David Bernstein does, "Is there a market in the gap?" Not "What's the problem?" but "Where's the opportunity in the problem?"

MARKETING GURUS

Marketing, like all pseudo-professions, takes its academic gunslingers very seriously.

It is definitely useful to know a little about marketing's Hot Gospellers and indeed it is very fashionable to beachcomb for interesting bits of conceptual flotsam and jetsam washed up at conferences. But deploy such learning with care: the best way of concept dropping is with a degree of cynicism. Most marketing people have a love-hate relationship with clever thinking. They love their own and hate everybody else's.

Here are small number of carefully chosen gurus with a note on their work.

Theodore Levitt

Levitt (or Ted, if you want to impress your audience and suggest the excellence of your marketing credentials) has been intimately associated with the Harvard Business Review (HBR to the initiated) and is a leading professor at the school. He is probably the most able apologist of the Marketing Concept, and the skilled bluffer should nod approvingly of two seminal Levitt texts: *Marketing Myopia* (HBR, 1960) and *The Globalisation of Markets* (HBR, 1983).

Marketing Myopia is an essential piece of conceptualisation for all bluffers. It originated from Levitt's analysis of the decline and fall of the great American railroads. These suffered from myopia because they saw themselves as being in the railway business rather than the transportation business and so let all manner of new competitors steal their customers.

The principle of marketing myopia allows you to look quite impressive in meetings. In a serious development meeting, ask your colleagues what business they are

15

in. For example, supposing you work in marketing for a bank, possible answers to the question could be:

Banking. This should have been anticipated but keep at it anyway.

Retailing. An interesting possibility, but a short-term one, perhaps.

Information Technology. Make the clever so and so who said this say what it actually means.

Dreams (via credit and loans). Encourage this participant.

'Security' for people. This one will definitely go the distance. Watch out for your job.

Philip Kotler

Always referred to as 'Kotler' as in 'Roget's' or 'Wisden' but without the rude words of the former or the wit of the latter. You should claim to have read Kotler at some stage in your career because his not-so-slim volume is the standard vademecum for marketing students.

Kotler is sound but sedating. Only in *Marketing Management: Analysis, Planning and Control* will you find such classics as: Demarketing, Counter Marketing, Synchromarketing and Remarketing. Whatever they are.

Tom Peters

A McKinsey staffer long since gone global on the back of several best-selling books on 'excellence' (the first two written with Robert Waterman). Renowned for folksy wisdom, regular columns and one of the best day rates in the business. Remembered for saying – having made a fortune out of excellence – that there are no excellent companies. You might care to substitute strategists for companies.

16

Igor Ansoff

Another useful name to drop especially when discussing New Product Development (NPD). Ansoff is the author of *Corporate Strategy*, an immensely unreadable text with one or two good pictures. His diversification matrix differentiates between existing products and new products; and between existing markets and new markets. Putting the two together can provide hours of fun at awaydays.

Ansoff's Diversification Matrix

	Product	
	Existing	New
Existing Market	Penetration	Product Development
New Market	Line Extension	Diversification

Michael Porter

Another Harvard man reinforcing their dominant share in the marketing guru business. Porter is a specialist in analysing competitive forces. *Competitive Strategy* (1980) and *Competitive Advantage* (1985) will look good (i.e. intimidating) on your office shelves. But to espouse *The Competitive Advantage of Nations* may be going a bit far.

You can appear to be a Porterian by constantly referring to the 'value chain'.

MARKETING TYPES

There are three basic types of marketeers (and some of them are very basic). All are ageless, though the packaging may change with times. The problem is to decide which type is going to work best for you. Qualifications are irrelevant, as is knowledge. It's the conviction with which you play the rôle that is crucial.

The Academic

Regardless of educational background, you should behave as if you had had an Oxford, Cambridge or Ivy League education. Because so many marketeers did go to Oxbridge, Harvard, etc. it is dangerous to make too precise a claim. You will have studied History or English or Modern Languages, possibly a science subject – but not Economics.

You should read the marketing press openly and keep clippings from obscure marketing journals above your desk. You have, of course, read *In Search of Excellence* and its profitable sequels, but you will be well aware that today, in Peter's words, 'there are no excellent companies'. Your own interests, quite coincidentally, are turning towards Chaos Theory and the need for Continuous Innovation.

Academic marketing people don't *do* things (at least not without much research and many feasibility studies) but they are proud to be action-orientated. As an academic bluffer you will also have read the popular classics of business life like *Up the Organisation* and *What They Don't Teach at the Harvard Business School*, and you will pass off their practical wisdom as your own 'insights'.

You dress well (but not too formally), drive a Audi TT or a Merc (unless you're a very new New Man or Woman) and, if the conversation turns to sporting pastimes, admit to having fenced a little at college or played a spot of Real Tennis – but not recently. When you take holidays, you make it clear that they are taken not for the sake of entertainment or relaxation *per se* but to 'recharge your creative batteries'. Your heroes are Levitt and Porter and you will refer to them as your 'mentors'.

A sub-grouping of the academic is the **strategist**. The strategist shares most of the same behavioural traits as the academic but tends to be less showy and, if male, more addicted to drawing two-dimensional matrices.

As a strategist you should constantly ask your colleagues (and superiors) whether a particular action meets the agreed strategic objectives (never the strategy). Since there's a good chance that most people won't remember their corporate objectives (let alone their business mission) you score highly. All you need to know is that the actions of those who can help you and your career are 'on strategy'. The rest aren't.

You can bolster the impact of your questions by citing obscure analogies from military history. "Is this the Somme in early 1916?", you will enquire, "or perhaps the Sino-Manchurian conflict of 1905?" This is guaranteed to leave everyone else silent, particularly those who trained as historians, and the field will be clear to draw your own conclusions. But beware of too many definite answers. Strategy is about long-term issues not short-term action. Your hero may well be the Duke of Wellington: monosyllabic, down to earth and intolerant of fools.

The Action Man

Action man's credo was best summed up by William Casey, American millionaire, spymaster and conspirator: 'Set tasks. Set deadlines. Make decisions. Act. Get it done and move on.'

Education and background are irrelevant – except that the successful must acquire a curt and heavy-weight style of memo writing and the ability to delegate all the tasks to someone else.

As action man, you set the tasks and the deadlines. You take a great many decisions and take credit for a great deal of action. You then move on. This is crucial. Stay in one job a fraction too long and the consequences of the decisions and the actions may catch up.

Publicly you don't read the marketing press – you have no time. Instead you require your subordinates to go through the press with a hi-liter – a useful familiarisation exercise you feel, and one which is done solely for their benefit. In private you read the job advertisements with attention. If you allow yourself one piece of familiarity with the business gurus it may well be Peter Drucker's statement that 'concentration is the key to economic results'. Or, in the words of numberless consulting gurus, "Stick to your **core competences**" (i.e. 'stick to the knitting').

When you entertain you do so at smart but 'newly discovered' restaurants. You don't have time for holidays – except the occasional weekend skiing in Tahoe or windsurfing in Corsica.

Be careful about heroes. Rather too many candidates have gone bust or gone to jail. Or both. For a few (who will normally be much older and much more senior than you) and for them only, you will claim to have "a lot of time".

But not too much.

20

The Street Trader

Much the most difficult. You must have left school early, preferably after organising some highly profitable (and slightly dodgy) activity from the local telephone box. Ideally, you will have started with a street barrow; certainly you ascribe your success to a talent for trading. You will have made your way up from rags to riches (exaggerate both) by exercise of a powerful personality and a talent for spotting opportunities.

You pay absolutely no attention to market research or marketing theory. Your instinct (call it your "gut feeling") is what counts. You would, you say, much prefer to be out in the field selling or talking to the customers, than behind a desk. This provides the justification for a generous expense account which you spend on late-night entertainment for customers.

Your clothes are largely irrelevant but are certainly different. When you've made it, you will pilot your own helicopter. Until then you drive whatever comes to hand with a blatant disregard for other road users.

Your philosophy of marketing is to pile it high, make a lot of noise and sell it cheap. You won't care much about what product you deal with but you will threaten anyone who makes unfavourable comments about it. You reserve your greatest contempt for wimps of any variety. In your early days your holidays will be spent running another business on the side. This will probably make (or have already made) your first million. In later life you'll have the time and energy to get into highly conspicuous consumption.

Your heroes are the few remaining entrepreneurs of the 1980s and 90s still solidly on their feet. The pursuit of money and power may not be fashionable, but you don't care. They've still got a lot going for them.

21

THE MARKETING HIERARCHY

Managing Director/General Manager – Somebody who has transcended mere marketing into the upper management ether. Still likes to get involved occasionally, usually with your advertising. Treat with apparent respect.

Marketing Director – Usually your boss and the board member responsible for all marketing activities and personnel. Very popular with the mail due to the pile of love letters delivered daily from advertising agencies.

Director of Marketing – Deceptively similar to the above but not on the board of the company. In marketing jargon, a question mark or problem child.

Marketing Controller – Someone with the talent of a Marketing Manager and the vanity of a Marketing Director. Usually sublimates personal aggression into your expenses and the questioning thereof.

Category Manager – Someone who does the job of a Marketing Director but is paid as a Marketing Manager.

Marketing Manager – Group Product Manager with go-faster stripes.

Marketing Operations Manager – Invaluable ally or dangerous enemy. The person who makes sure everything happens on time, at the right price, and in the best hotels.

Brand Manager – Either the storm troopers of marketing or the Thin Red Line. 'Brand masochists' is another description.

Assistant Brand Manager – An endangered species. The position no-one ever admits to. Who would want to be an assistant oily rag?

Marketing Assistant – Graduate trainee with sales experience.

Graduate Trainee – Enthusiast with no experience. Usually the best informed about such trivia as sales volumes, customers, etc. This is because they're still keener on their jobs than their careers.

Marketing and its Interfaces

There are two sets of people to consider here. Those inside the company and those outside.

The Insiders

As a marketeer you see yourself at the centre of the organisational wheel. That goes without saying, though you recognise that there are still plenty of corporate luddites who don't see things your way.

The argument runs like this. Business is about meeting the needs of customers – at a profit. Therefore the customers and their needs must be at the centre of any profitable approach to business. Support for this view comes from Hugh Davidson who defined marketing as the 'total approach to business which places the consumer at the centre of things'. Two other good quotes are: 'Markets don't pay bills, customers do' and 'Customers make pay day possible'. Thus you should be setting the strategy, you should be controlling the production and directing the sales people and the accountants should be advising you on how to do so profitably. Unfortunately they don't usually see it that way. Conflict is the name of the game. It's called office politics.

The conflict with **Sales** is usually the bitterest. This is because it's a class issue. It used to be secondary modern kids against the grammar school swots. Now it's probably university versus business school types.

You have two courses of action with sales people:

1. Be publicly aggressive and privately one of the lads. This should enable you to get away unscathed with dirty deeds.

2. Advocate the integration of sales and marketing. This is shorthand for marketing telling the sales people what to do – but 'integration' sounds better.

Dealing with **Production** is less of a problem. Nobody pays them much attention because nobody these days wants to be thought a 'product-led' company. This can be a dangerous attitude. Quality control and technical feasibility are very important to any marketing concept when it hits the real world. You should insist that your people 'take pride in the product' and, in public at least, you should do so yourself. It will win you a lot of points and it should make the production director your ally (which can be a very good thing indeed).

Active conflict with the **Accountants** is dangerous. Corporate finance directors still carry a lot of clout – particularly in companies where share options are part of the package.

In private you can dismiss them as 'bean-counters' and point to the ineptitude of the American car industry in the face of Japanese competition as an example of what happens when accountants get their inky fingers on the levers of power.

In public adopt the 'hard man'/'soft man' approach. On the one hand beat them over the head with reams of market research data. On the other, appeal to their entrepreneurial instincts (if they have any). Go for the Big Idea. Even if you don't convince the accountants you'll impress everyone else.

Finally, two groups of in-house people you must always have on your side:

1. Secretaries – invaluable for fixing impossible meetings, providing inside information on the boss's state of mind, fending off unwanted phone calls, booking the best hotels and bending the rules.

2. Whoever has the key to the corporate cocktail cabinet.

The Outsiders

Agencies present one sort of problem; you have to pay them. Agencies range from good to awful but this doesn't make much difference to their price – particularly if you're operating on a commission basis. (The theory was, and still is, that the agency costs you nothing because they get a discount on the media space they buy for you, and then charge you the same amount as their commission. If you believe that you'll believe anything.)

The important thing is to get the best available operators and get the most out of them. They exist to serve you. Remember that. This doesn't necessarily mean that they will do what you want but they should always be prepared to humour your incidental wishes on the subject of good contacts, lunch, entertainment, introductions to desirable young account executives, alternative jobs and so forth. They may even be willing to hire you.

The one exception to this rule is Market Research Agencies. Ethics, professional codes of conduct and less money mean they don't appear such an accommodating bunch. There are three things to remember about market research agencies:

1. Make sure they know what results you expect before they start work (or at least before they write their reports).

2. Insist that there is a 'management summary' at the front of the report. (This should definitely say what you want them to say.)

3. Ensure that they put the unwanted bits somewhere around page 297. Nobody will ever see them there.

Consumers and **customers** present another sort of problem. You have to get them to pay you.

Consumers are the subject of fascinated study by armies of marketeers, market research companies and advertising agencies. You need to be aware of what 'real' people are currently doing and thinking. This is the justification, if any were needed, for reading the *Sun*, studying the Agony columns or the letters pages of top shelf magazines, buying bottles of champagne or ready meals. Whatever takes your fancy in fact. The trick is to ensure that all such diversions go down on your expenses sheet as 'product samples' or 'market research' expenses.

Qualitative research groups are always a source of good consumer anecdotes. It may help you to know, for example, that 17-year-old headbangers know more about the contents and containers of every conceivable form of alcohol than you ever will.

Customers may also be consumers. But not necessarily. More often than not customers are retailers and their customers are your consumers. Not everyone has caught up with this obvious fact. Not everyone has got used to new ways of dealing with customers.

Consumer marketing used to be the focus of manufacturers' marketing activity. But now major retailers have established their own branded identities and the new idea is Trade Marketing.

Trade marketing is about applying the same standard of research, rigour and creativity to the trade as old-style marketing departments did to the consumer. Having applied that effort, the challenge is to create long-term relationships with the trade in the same way as Lever Brothers did with its Persil mums. That means understanding the needs of the trade and getting away from relationships that are based solely on today's special offer. They don't last.

Tell anyone who insists on low prices to remember 'winners compete by delivering a product that supplies superior values to customers rather than one that costs less'. Above all, avoid the trap of Marketing Myopia. Think 'customers' rather than 'consumers' when it comes to developing new products, assessing communication channels or commissioning research.

An associated trap is Consumerism. Don't believe everything consumers say to you. Some of the most successful product launches have been those which flew in the face of all the research evidence – and vice versa. If you're launching a new product you can always claim that consumers are slow to appreciate something they don't already know about.

Conversely, score points by asking "Where's the real product difference?" Research on NPD does show that if the product does not have such a difference, its chances are pretty slim. It all goes to prove that the big idea is best.

WHAT MARKETEERS DO

1. Develop Market Plans

Marketeers, like politicians, come in a variety of hues and views. And just as all politicians have to face election from time to time, marketeers have to get through marketing plans. In fact these activities are very similar – both involve rehashing the past and over-promising the future.

The future is very important to marketing, something which sets it aside from finance. Superficially, a marketing plan is a bit like a balance sheet or profit and loss account, but whilst the P & L and balance sheet are snapshots relating to the past, the marketing plan is a vision of the future.

It is easy to get excited about a vision of the future – especially when it happens to be yours – but always remember that visions stretch credibility, especially with Chief Executives who have seen it all before. Be very careful with the 'expansiveness of your perspective'.

Marketing plans come in a number of guises:

- Annual Brand Plan
- Market Strategy
- Budget

and will have varying time horizons: 1 year/2 years/3 years/5 years/10 years. The longer the range of plan, the longer the odds on anybody taking it seriously.

Marketing plans also bring out different things in marketing people. Action men hate the annual navel-gazing activity as much as the academic loves to work up a sweat with a **SWOT chart** or a juicy little **matrix**.

Most marketing textbooks will tell you that good planning only emerges from rigorous analysis of the key questions about the business. But what bluffers should be asking are:

The Open Questions	The Hidden Questions
Where are we now?	For a start, why am I here now?
How did we get there?	Who is to blame and why has he got a bigger car?
Where do we want to be?	Never mind 'we'. Where do *I* want to be?
How do we get there?	How do I get my CV typed without the boss seeing it?

Marketing planning depends on a number of key concepts. The chief one is:

Segmentation

'If you're not thinking segments, you're not thinking marketing.' Ted Levitt said that, and it's worth remembering. This does not mean dismembering your Marketing Director into his or her component parts – tempting though that may be.

The consumers in a market, any market, have different needs (**need states**) which can be satisfied by different products or different positionings of similar (or even identical) products. Split your market into groups of customers:

- by age
- by life-cycle stage (an impressive way of talking about the differences between, say, those who are married and those who are not)
- by attitudes to using credit cards, or
- by any combination of the above and a hundred other attributes.

29

Instantly you have a segmentation. You are limited only by your imagination and that of your agency.

Agencies (or rather their planning departments) compete for new and more 'focused' (read elaborate) segmentations of each and every market.

You should know that Hugh Davidson describes segmentation as a 'touchstone for offensive marketing'. Segmentation is a powerful tool for:

- new product development;
- maximising the potential of existing brands, and
- avoiding cannibalisation (winning sales at your expense rather than that of your competitors).

But beware of segmenting the market so finely that you finish up with a host of separate market sectors that are too small to attack profitably.

Key segmentation variables are:

a) demographics

b) usage level, and

c) personality or lifestyle factors (don't use the word psychographic unless your ambition is to be thought intellectual and old fashioned).

Some people would include value – effectively a segmentation around various price points – but this does not help to understand the market. There are two key questions to ask of any segmentation.

1. Does this segmentation help us to understand our customers better and market to them more effectively?

2. Is the segmentation supported by data? Listen hard to the answers for the sounds of evasive action.

The Product Life-Cycle

The easy way of explaining why your sales are disappearing. That's the defensive use. The offensive use is to ask what stage of its life-cycle a given product has reached. Whatever the answer ignore it and ask about the product portfolio mix (q.v).

You'll know, of course, that it's based on the sensible and realistic idea that every product goes through:

a) a period of development (high costs, low revenue and low profit)

b) a period of growth (rapidly rising sales and profits)

c) a period of maturity (highest sales but declining profit margin as competitors come in and prices tend to fall); and finally

d) a period of decline (consumers shift to new products, competition intensifies, sales and profits drop away).

You will also know – and gently point out – that it seems that nobody told Mars about it. Or Kelloggs. Or Heinz. Or a number of other marketing-centred companies that know the value of powerful brands.

Products certainly have a life-cycle. Brands needn't have. Even the seemingly moribund can be renewed and repositioned. You can quote the case history of Lucozade as a perfect example of this truism. From being the old fashioned bedside tonic for invalids it became, with Olympic Decathlete Daley Thompson's assistance, the energy drink.

New brands are hard to create which explains why self-styled shrewd operators are still willing to spend a lot of money buying old brands. A good question to ask about anybody's brands, except your own, is "But are they real brands?" Very often they aren't.

Portfolio Planning

This, as all strategically minded bluffers know very well, used to be very sexy stuff indeed: 'a major task of top management'. It provided the excuse for elegant matrices and made a lot of money for the Boston Consulting Group. It is still pretty powerful and you should appear to know all about it.

Business or brands are plotted against the twin axes of market growth rate and relative market share. You therefore get four quadrants – each with its complement of **SBUs** (Strategic Business Units):

Stars – Fast growth and high market share.

Cash cows – Low growth rate but high share.

Dogs – Low growth rate and low market share.

Problem Children or **Question Marks** – Low share but high rate of market growth.

The question is do you join in enthusiastically or launch an attack? Either is possible. If you want to join in, talk earnestly about the strategy for each SBU or brand: build, hold, harvest or divest. Hit back by using the diffusion curve to interrogate colleagues about the product life-cycle stage.

If you want to attack then the best route is to question the principle of diversification which underlies this and other similar portfolio strategies. Suggest that the company "stick to the knitting". Deprecate the mental set that such portfolio analysis produces. Refer to Peters and Waterman's analysis of their 'excellent companies'. They didn't think much of diversification and the **Boston Matrix**. It wasn't their consulting group who invented it.

The Boston Group Matrix:

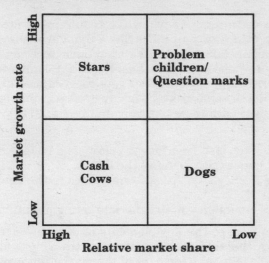

If someone else is attacking the idea of portfolio analysis you remind them that ICI used a similar approach to earn a 'better billion'. Suggest that you too see merit in earning a 'better' million or a 'better' dollar. Nobody can argue with you, but nobody. Then point out that this is a *strategic* issue and what's good enough for ICI should do pretty well for most of the rest of us.

If it's a question of products or brands, tread more cautiously. If you're an academic or a strategist then you should support portfolio planning wholeheartedly (though don't forget to express belief in the power of your brands). Only if you're an out and out action man or street trader can you afford to differ. Even then you're probably better off denying all specialised knowledge and saying the same things in the most down to earth vocabulary you can find.

The Emergency Matrix

There are certain times when the requirement for a marketing plan hits your office like a thunderbolt from Zeus. It might, for example, be an unannounced visit from the Vice-President North-East Regional Coordinator for Western Europe, who never gets chart-lagged and positively loves comparing your advertising campaign to that of the Venezuelan company. In this situation you can:

1. Repeat the last marketing plan and hope he doesn't notice (risky, to say the least).
2. Get the agency to do a new one (comes to the same thing as (1).
3. Use this emergency matrix for marketing planning.

Across the top are the key elements of the marketing mix. Down the side is a list of verbs covering what you can do about each element of the marketing mix.

Strategy   Marketing mix

	Product	Price	Promotion	Place	Positioning	Packaging
innovate						
imitate						
adopt						
adapt						
ignore						
hold						
improve						
enter						
harvest						
exit						

Take a number of copies of the matrix, prepared for overhead projection, into your meeting along with a selection of different colour OHP pens.

Announce to the group that as the brand-planning process is a continuous cycle, you would like to lead a brainstorming where each strategy is rated one out of ten for effectiveness in regard to each element of the mix. Comparisons with Venezuela are the subject of another acetate, of course, and should be encouraged.

After about five minutes of your presentation, everybody should start arguing – led by the Vice President. Sit back with your spare matrix and mark it up according to the direction of the meeting. After about 45 minutes, announce that you'd like to summarise the discussion thus far and to examine the chosen strategies in more detail.

Present the chart and a series of agreed next steps and then sit down. With a bit of luck you will have saved yourself – and the agency – a week's work. Note this only works once.

Marketing Economics

It is essential to be familiar with the financial jargon you will come across in marketing plans and budgets. The most important are:

Sales volume – Your brand's sales in units: could be litres, cases, barrels, boxes or kilograms.

Sterling sales at RSP – What your brand actually turned over.

Net Sale Volume (NSV) – What your company actually received, less discounts.

Gross contribution – NSV less the 'variable costs'.

Net contribution – Gross contribution less 'fixed costs' e.g. heating, lighting, the rental of the corporate HQ and the Chairman's yacht.

Contribution after marketing – What your brand actually puts into the corporate pot.

Breakeven point – Where NSV equals variable plus fixed costs. From here on in you're into profit.

Profit Margin – usually
$\frac{\text{PBIT}}{\text{sales}}$ or $\frac{\text{PBIT}}{\text{NSV}}$ expressed as a percentage.

2. Commission Market Research

Marketing is an information technology and you can't market blind. Well you can, and most marketeers do so from time to time, but in order to do without market research you need to know a little about it.

Because marketing is consumption orientated, the process of meeting needs has been likened to the motion of a boomerang. The return trip happens to be the wedge of research data that whacks you on the head after asking simple questions about what the consumer wants. So beware of asking simple questions.

Market research is the petrol of marketing: it's expensive, damaging to the environment and will only take you so far. This has not prevented it from becoming one of the boom industries. There are of course many different types of market research and the field is characterised by a high degree of semi-masonic jargon designed to put off the lay marketing person.

Do not be put off. The best strategy is to deploy

common sense to penetrate the cloud of un-meaning which tends to hover over most research proposals.

The basic types of market research you should know about are:

Quantitative – (Latin 'quanto' meaning by how much?) This usually involves counting observations amongst large samples of people and is usually expressed via percentages. A typical quantitative finding might be: *'17% of housewives like stuffing.'*

Qualitative – (Latin 'qualis' meaning of what kind, sort or nature?) This method seeks not to measure rigorously but rather to 'explore' attitudes and motivations in depth among small samples of people. A typical finding might be: *'stuffing users are inward looking social adventurers.'*

Until recently, quantitative researchers have been the underdogs, beavering away in obscurity. Their reports were often telling but irredeemably tedious. By contrast, qualitative researchers have enjoyed the limelight with sexy research techniques that involved video cameras and bottles of wine and provided lots of good stories about suburban housewives and the social mores of C2s.

There are (or were) two main reasons for this ascendancy. Firstly their style. As a group, qualitative researchers tend to be personable, intelligent, fluent talkers and good listeners. They therefore find it easy to bluff their way in marketing. Remember this. You are buying the interpretative (and marketing) skills of one or two people. If they are good hang on to them – if not discard them ruthlessly, regardless of the quality of their presentations. You will often find an inverse relationship – the more glossy the report, the more hackneyed the thinking.

Secondly, their viewpoint. Qualitative research at its best is about tomorrow. It is thought-provoking, relevant and extremely difficult to disprove. By contrast, quantitative research has traditionally been about yesterday. What did people do yesterday (or last month or last year)? But that's changing fast. Quantitative research is hitting back and anyone willing to bluff their way in new technology can now score heavily. Be reassured – you don't need to know anything about the techniques. What you do need is a few useful concepts.

The best is the idea of **modelling**, putting together a computer 'model' of how a particular group of people behave. Once the model is set up you can ask endless 'what if?' questions.

Another useful computer application is ultra-fine **targeting** for direct selling of any form. New technology and nifty software enables you to locate not just the towns and districts in which your target market is likely to live but also the individual streets.

Continuous surveys are the major studies clients buy on a regular basis in order to measure markets, retailer purchases, consumer sales and changes in consumer attitudes.

Retail audit presentations are usually good for a slanging match between sales and marketing. This is because the figures are always believed to be too low by one side and too high by the other side. Try for a ringside seat but avoid being caught in the clinches.

Consumer panels allow you to explore consumer dynamics. You do not need to know what this means, only that it's what panels are good for.

Tracking studies are used to beat advertising agencies over the head when they reveal a pathetic unprompted awareness score for your product.

(Unprompted awareness is what sorts out the real winners – it's all too easy to tell a researcher you've heard of a name on a card. After all you don't want to sound like someone who spends the commercial breaks making cups of tea.)

Ad hoc is the term used to describe any survey conducted to meet specific research objectives on a marketing problem not covered in continuous surveys. Ad hoc research can be quantitative or qualitative, premium or bargain basement. When you think about commissioning an ad hoc survey consider this: 'If you need it, you can't use it' and 'If you can use it, you don't need it'. The development of this rule is: 'The usefulness of any research is not measured by its inherent quality but by the ability of those on the receiving end to do something about it.'

In-house Market Researchers

Always treat your in-house researchers with a mixture of caution and respect because:

a) Unlike outside researchers you don't pay their wages (at least, not usually). This means that they are not as subservient as they might otherwise be.

b) They can get very uppity about research, especially when you flout its findings (i.e. *their* findings).

c) They can help you cut through the waffle, buy effectively and make the results comprehensible.

On balance, it is always worth keeping researchers on your side, encouraging them to take up a 'planning stance' on your brand. This will go down very well.

39

Market Research Jargon

Acorn: A Classification of Residential Neighbourhoods – Who lives where.

MOSAIC – The same but different.

TNS – Research agency obsessed with the rubbish in people's dustbins. All of us, one day, will be on a TNS panel.

TGI: Target Group Index – Survey much loved by the media to demonstrate that their organ is read by more blue cheese dressing users than anyone else.

TAT: Thematic Apperception Test – Getting consumers to describe their feelings with crayons and paper.

CATI: Computer Assisted Telephone Interviewing – Resting place for out of work actors to practise their interpersonal communication skills via the telephone directory.

EPOS: Electronic point of sale – Bar coding.

EFTPOS: Electronic Funds Transfer at Point of Sale – Talk about whether the cashless society is a reality.

IMPOS: Impossible – The consequences of EPOS/ EFTPOS on those who have to analyse the data.

STM: Simulated Test Market – Fashionable method of testing the marketing mix.

BAR Test – Not as promising as it sounds. Benefit and Reason Why Test. Popular with Procter & Gamble.

DAR: Day After Recall – Advertising testing technique on which to pour scorn, unless employed by P+G.

CUT – Consumer Usage Test. A.k.a. **CLT**, Central Location Test, the opposite of a home placement test.

DPP – Direct Product Profitability. What the trade uses to beat margins down.

Projective Techniques – Market research meets improvisation. If Heineken could talk to Budweiser, what would it say?

ECG: Extended Creativity Groups – Expensive entertaining with consumers and plenty of TATs.

ABC1C2DE or **SEGs** (Socio-Economic Groupings) – As are judges and generals, Bs are marketeers (except Directors), C1s inspect your tax returns, C2s install your central heating, Ds remove your rubbish and Es are elderly parents and spendthrift youth at university.

NRS: National Readership Survey – Major study of press readership. How many papers did you look at yesterday?

OTS: Opportunities to see – the average number of times the target audience is supposed to see your ad.

OTT – Usual cost of generating sufficient OTS.

3. Launch New Products

It is proverbial amongst marketing people that new products are a company's lifeblood. It is less obvious that marketeers frequently spill blood (their own included) to make new product development happen.

Only 1 in 20 new products succeed, which means that 19 out of 20 new products and their managers fail. As a successful bluffer you will want to make your career, not break it. What follows, therefore, are the success factors for career development via new products.

a) Ideas are not the problem

Getting ideas is not the issue. You'll find ideas at exhibitions, during the essential yearly trips to Japan or simply by looking at your competitors' catalogues. You can even spend very pleasant awaydays with the agency brainstorming new concepts.

The real problem you have to address is finding the right ideas. In the 1970s many companies headed lemming-like into 'kettle technology' (a.k.a. pot snacks). Huge investment in plant and technology followed, the market proved to be a can of worms and the inevitable shakedown resulted. Home computers and games software was a similar story. Ditto **NABLABS** (No Alcohol and Low Alcohol Beers).

As a general rule, then, avoid fashion markets. By the time they start generating interest in the press, it's too late for you to do anything useful apart from knocking the idea on the head.

b) Know what the company is actually good at

Not many companies are able to change their characteristics overnight. You will therefore stand a much better chance of picking a project with potential if you understand the assets and liabilities of your company.

A key concept to raise when your MD discusses diversification is the idea of 'the experience curve barrier to entry'. This means that if you have never ridden a bicycle before, the chances are that you will end up sitting on the floor looking foolish.

c) Get a product champion

Academic research has revealed the importance of a product champion to new product success. This excludes your spouse, your mother and your agency

Account Director. The product champion is a very senior company executive who believes in your project and can help you cut through the politics and get decisions taken. Great care, however, should be taken when the project champion happens to be the MD and the product is his pet project.

d) Never underestimate the workload

Setting up a new business is extremely time-consuming. When a product has no history everybody in the organisation has to be educated about it. Given the lead times involved in capital expenditure, plant, trials, packaging and advertising, it is sensible to have plenty of help on hand. If this is not available in-house, use an agency to do the legwork.

e) Decide a clear rôle for market research

Full rigour product development consists of lots of market research stages. Any or all of the following could be used:

- early 'exploratory' qualitative research
- concept research in groups
- home placement or hall test surveys
- advertising development research
- packaging research
- test marketing (e.g. STM)

When commissioning research and spending the company's money decide what your motivations are. Do you want to:

1. Blow the project out of the water?
2. Get the product to market by hook or by crook?
3. Satisfy a spirit of enquiry?

f) **Develop a new brand** (not just a new product)

Remember that companies may **make** products, but consumers **buy** brands.

g) **Sell it to the sales force**

The hardest test of any new product and by far the trickiest hurdle to negotiate is the response of the sales force. Since they have such an unpleasant job being nice to buyers who are not nice to them they enjoy the rôle reversal. You are selling, they are buying and they make it difficult.

Do not put your faith in lasers and pretty slides: put yourself in their shoes. It's a wet Monday morning and you are sitting in a bleak reception with 27 other salesmen drinking undrinkable coffee. Now what are the real benefits of the product?

h) **Watch the first few days of the launch carefully**

Just as the television pollsters can predict the winner's majority in the General Election from the first few declarations, so you can judge whether this project is your responsibility or someone else's from:

• the results of the first trade presentations.
• consumer purchasing rates and repeat buying from panel data and ad hoc surveys.

Post launch research can be highly useful but there is a delicate balance to be struck between saving your own skin or finding out how you can do better next time.

Note: whilst large NPD successes are the products of many fathers, you will rarely meet a marketing person who has launched a failure.

i) **Avoid the effects of failure**

- Deny the failure entirely ("We achieved 75% sterling distribution in the North-East").
- Blame Production (or Sales) for crimes unspecified.
- Blame the retailers for bringing out an own label six weeks after launch. (Always a good one – particularly if it's true.)
- Blame the company for failing to realise the necessity of serious media spending.
- Philosophise on the problems (and costs) of creating a 'real' brand these days.
- Vigorously affirm the importance of taking big risks for big rewards. A host of 'me-toos' doesn't help anybody very much.
- Stress the problems inherent in 'discontinuous innovations' (i.e. really new ideas). The implication is that you have had the courage to think big and bet big.
- Cite other new product failures (the Sinclair C5, the Ford Edsel, new smoking materials, TVP food products). On second thoughts, don't.
- Find another job before anyone has noticed what has happened.

New Product Jargon

Added value – What most new products claim to have. Generic claim in sales presentations and sales presenters. Excuse for a high price.

Blind Test – A consumer test without identifying the product.

Concept/Product Fit – Getting it right. Harder than it looks.

Existing Products (OPD) – Making the most of existing brand assets, e.g. stretching the brand name into new territories. Now a whole new field of NPD.

Insulation – Attempt to provide barriers to competitors in the market targeted by your new product.

Kill point – Termination at the worst possible moment.

Me-too – Competitive entrant in your new market.

Me-too late – What you would never be guilty of launching.

Insight – Fashionable name for research. The blindingly obvious dressed as deep illumination.

Roll-out – The extension of a product out of its test market area. Not to be confused with roll up.

STM – Trendy kind of test market. Expensive, but liked by Marketing Directors.

Funnel and gates – To get good ideas you need lots of ideas which you 'feed into a funnel'; the gates are the research hurdles your idea has to pass.

Three Ts of Innovation:

Twinkles – Major breakthroughs. High risk and high return, e.g. Quorn, CD Roms and Compuserve. Chairmen love them unless they're paying.

Twists – Clever marketing sleight of hand which results in paying more for the same thing, e.g. Pepsi Max which repositioned artificially sweetened drinks as drinks for men rather than as diet drinks.

Tweaks – Anti-dandruff, hedgehog-flavour line extensions. A bit sad, distinctly uncreative but both necessary and – occasionally – very profitable.

4. Brand Things

What is Branding?

The process of communicating with the customer is the bit most marketeers enjoy the most; developing their skill and talent in the serious art of **branding**.

There is a world of difference between a product and a brand; between Ribes Nigrum and Ribena; between ordinary denims and Levi 501s; between cat food and Whiskas. Products are generic; brands are unique.

Classical branding is a semi-religious activity requiring much respect for and worshipping of the brand values which have been created and reinforced over time. Brand values are a mixture of functional factors like price, performance and, say, taste and the emotional values connoted by the brand name, the style of its advertising and the properties of the package: the Oxo Mum.

The reason why marketeers take branding so seriously is that branding is about the security of future profits. It is relatively easy to get a single sale, it is far more efficient to create a pattern of loyalty somewhat resembling inertia selling. It is much easier to defend a brand which has far more dimensions to differentiate it than a commodity. Smash and its Martians were far more defensible than Cadbury Instant Mash Potato.

Branding brings other benefits too. Having created a distinctive image with consumers, brands can be extended within their area of authority. Richard Branson's racket busting, consumer's champion concept has been applied across airlines, cola, vodka, showergel, mortgages, and cross country trains.

Where brands are extended beyond their 'franchise', or where brand values are diluted by inconsistent advertising messages or investment, brands can easily lay themselves open to attack from other manufacturer brands, or even, in the case of FMCG, the retailer's own brand, which in these days of retailer marketing and power, are some of the most powerful around.

Bluffers should treat retailer brands with care.

Positioning

If brand values are the sum total of the physical and psychological attributes of a product, positioning is the word for how that brand is focused against the marketplace and its competitors. Good bluffers will display elegant positioning thinking. There is a really easy 'positioning template' you can have ready for action at all times:

'Only Brandname gives (insert target group) (insert benefit) because only Brandname has / contains / does (insert reason why).' As in:

'Only Bloggo Spray gives Merry Wives of Windsor a kitchen aroma they can be proud of because only Bloggo contains the essence of real Provençal lavender.'

The best positioning is that which is both consistent with brand values and most effectively touches the consumer's nerve.

Products in different markets can have differing positionings, though many global marketeers seek to avoid this. As markets evolve or change in nature, a product can be repositioned (see Product Life-Cycle).

Most marketeers will run into positioning issues at some time. So here is a positioning checklist to get you off to an impressive start. Simply check the relevance of each idea as a platform for your brand.

Prestige	Excitement	Fashion	Sophistication
Fun	Mystery	Tradition	Convenience
Health	Romance	Bargain	Individual

But beware of 'positioning' statements that are merely meaningless straplines. 'Tomorrow's finest food today', for instance, says nothing. Over-use in the marketing mill has robbed the words of all meaning.

5. Make Presentations

Whatever their personal style all successful presenters are consummate bluffers. At least one celebrated ad agency chairman made a career out of apparently spontaneously throwing his notes away after a slide was deliberately shown out of order and successfully eliciting the response 'What a guy! How *did* he do that?'

The whole art of successful presentation is bluff. Expensive courses on presentation put it slightly differently, but that's what they mean.

Firstly, the content. This is the least important bit. It is not what you say but how you say it. Go for short, pithy generalisations – a few words to each slide or chart. Intersperse these with heavyweight numbers charts which you pass over arrogantly as an example of the work you have done. Then turn rapidly to the three-bullet point summary. Consider providing a back-up Databook which will remain an unread and reassuring presence after the meeting.

Expend your effort on commanding your audience. David Ogilvy always recommended reading every word on the chart exactly as it was written. He believed, probably rightly, that most of the audience were rarely awake enough to cope with two different messages coming at them. You acknowledge the truth of his remark but flatter this audience by crediting them with the capacity to be able to read and listen at the same time. They can't, but it should help to confuse them.

Insist that the presentation is rehearsed – with *all the material* that you'll use. Otherwise Murphy's Law will undoubtedly strike. This is crucial. There is no point in unnecessarily putting yourself in situations where you have to bluff to stay alive.

6. Buy Advertising

Agency People

Receptionist – Easily the most powerful person in the agency. Probably knows more about your account than the Account Director.

Chairman – Interesting cross-breed of public school housemaster and the Invisible Man.

Managing Director – The agency boss. Usually features in meetings when the agency has something to gain or to lose. Asking for his comments on the latest Nielsen should stop him in his tracks.

Creative Director – High earner, high profile and high style. Getting ever younger, like policemen.

Account Director – Living proof that opposites attract. Probably a defrocked marketeer. Treat with a mixture of suspicion and sympathy.

Account Planner – Smart-arse who turns your brief into baby talk for the creative department. Watch out when they feel a matrix coming on.

Account Manager – Usually a nice person who gets it in the neck from everybody. Still, this is advertising and it is your money.

Creative Team – The group whose function it is to create, and they do so frequently, but not necessarily advertisements. Watch them turn your product into gold and silver – usually D & AD Awards.

Traffic – The liquid engineering which keeps the creative department running smoothly.

Media Planners – Often second class citizens in agencies who compensate by engrossing themselves in TVRs, OTS, frequency schedules and response functions. By far the nicest crowd to have a drink with and you get invited to places like the Bahamas for conferences about 'Whither Television?'

Media Buyers – The ones who buy time from TV contractors and play a demon mixture of poker and chess. They can save you (or lose you) a lot of money. Don't be fooled by the accent or the beer consumption.

Pitching Etiquette

One of the most curious rituals of advertising is the elaborate courtship behaviour which develops between you, the client, and agencies seeking your business.

As an advanced bluffer, you will realise the necessity of observing certain customs and practices when you ask agencies to present their credentials. (The word comes from the latin, credo, meaning 'I believe'. Cynics might say 'incredentials' is a more accurate description.)

a) Do not laugh spontaneously and out loud as the agency presents its philosophy or says it doesn't have one. Agencies take philosophy very seriously and hours of client time are expended developing such classics as: 'We prefer to work in partnership with our clients' or 'We offer unique total communications solutions'.

b) It is accepted behaviour to show neutral body language in the course of the presentation, revealing neither interest nor boredom. An occasional note on the agency pad with the agency pen is a good ploy. This is a good time to compile your action list for the morrow.

c) When the case histories have finished, pass no judgement, give no praise, say "Thank you for that" and ask them a really heavy duty marketing question like: "How many parking spaces for clients do you have?"

d) Then ask them a vaguely relevant question like: "Do you think brands can recapture share from private label?" After about 20 minutes of live brainstorming by the agency say: "Thank you, that was useful."

e) To close the meeting, ask to meet the people who would actually work on the account. Then pick up whatever goodies are available and leave. Remember this is your moment of greatest power. It's downhill all the way from here.

High Noon at the Agency

Once you have correctly played the mating game, you have to get down to the mundane task of getting the advertising out of the agency. Getting your advertising

is not as easy as it seems. You may be absolutely
certain that this is what will happen:

1. You will discover that the campaign your
   Managing Director liked 'bombs' in research and
   there are just six weeks to the Sales Conference
   and twelve weeks to the national launch.

2. You will uncover an omission in the section of the
   agency's presentation dealing with the lead time
   for commercials.

3. You will receive a document from the planner
   entitled 'First Thoughts on an Approach to the
   Creative Brief'.

None of this is reassuring. Nor is the Account
Director's quip that Beethoven's Ninth was not
written overnight. Resist the temptation to point out
that Mozart usually wrote a symphony before break-
fast. It will get a good laugh but no action. Good
bluffers know that shock tactics are required.
Arrange a meeting between you, the MD or
Marketing Director and the agency boss. Energise the
whole agency by threatening:

a) Not to sign the agency's contract

b) Not to commit to media expenditure

c) To use a creative hotshop to do the work

d) To get a media independent to buy the media at
   reduced rates of commission.

e) To ring up *Campaign*.

This will get you your ads, but the next question is
what do they mean when they are presented to you?

Breaking Agency Codes

What They Say	*What they Mean*
Strategically sound.	Boring ad.
Well branded.	Very boring ad.
An idea so simple.	Extremely boring ad.
The product as hero is old hat.	We think the product is crap.
We think 'X' (a noted personality) says so much about the brand.	The product really *is* crap.
It blew their minds in research.	Consumers think the product is crap.
The product is very distinctive.	It's outrageous.
It's highly campaignable.	We can make even *more* on production.
It'll work in the press.	They can't afford television.
It's ideal for television.	There's a big budget here.
We've done a 60-second and a 30-second version.	Bet the nurd will go for the 30.
Make two for the price of one.	Make one for the price of two.
Look how we really built on your existing property.	But we had to level it first.
Imagine the trade ad.	We hope you can because we can't.
The Agency view is...	We don't agree.

7. **Promote Sales**

They also serve who sales promote. Good Sales Promotions agencies can make your money work extremely hard. They are more effective at gaining trial, generating sales and creating product loyalty than any of the other agencies you may choose to use.

Original ideas are a help – so long as they don't land you in court for infringing one or more of the many laws that govern sales promotions in general. Good ideas, old and new, are probably a better bet. Nobody ever won national recognition through their innovative sales promotions.

Good ideas are those which cost little, are easy to manage, keep the retailers sweet and meet your objectives. Be clear in your own mind what exactly you want to do. Against the consumer you may wish to:

- Gain trial
- Grab short-term volume
- Switch to larger packs
- Reward loyal users

Against the retailer the major objectives are to:

- Get more stock in
- Get trial
- Encourage staff awareness of your product
- Nobble the competition

Finally, there are the million and one incentive schemes to ginger up your sales force.

Sales promotions are about noise – creating it and cutting through it. Remember that there's a sort of Hawthorne Effect: it doesn't matter what you do as long as you keep changing things. In a series of experiments in America in the 1930s, industrial psychologist Elton Mayo discovered that brighter lights and louder music pushed up production line productivity. He also discovered that lower lights and quieter music had exactly the same effect. The change was what mattered. It made people feel they were being looked after, that an effort was being made on their behalf. This, by the way, includes bosses.

Incidentally, Hawthorne refers to the place not the psychologist. Not many people know that. Fewer care.

Promotion Jargon

Banded offers – The promotional equivalent of the blind date.

BOGOF – Buy One and Get One Free.

Competitions – The lifeblood of sales promotions. Watch out for the heavy hand of the law if there's not at least some element of skill.

Extra product – 33% more. Unfortunately at least 33% of the population don't understand just what that percentage increase *means*.

Collector devices – Blackmail to buy more.

Collaborative cross-product offers – Two manufacturers in bed together.

Price reductions – Short-term sales boost at the expense of your brand personality and image.

Shelf talkers – How to maximise every square inch of promotional space.

SLPs: Self Liquidating Promotions – a) a promotion that fires up the consumer and pays for itself; b) a promotion that fires everyone else (say Hoover and hope it doesn't happen to you).

Through the line – Even more expensive than Above or Below the line. See also Integrated – where you can't disentangle the bills.

Wobblers – Store decoration at your expense.

8. Exploit PR

Like Sales Promotions operations, PR agencies can be divided into those with good ideas and those with no ideas at all. Good PR can cost very little, bad PR can cost you and your brand a fortune. The trick is to pick the right one.

PR agencies come in a variety of shapes and sizes. Those who boast of their 'strategic' thinking will want to explain your own marketing plan to you. Those who offer 'total communications solutions' want to do your advertising as well.

To get the most out of your agency you should:

1. Make sure the agency puts both an ideas person and an organiser on your team. Plenty of agencies bubble over with bright ideas, but can't deliver on time, to specification or within budget. Others can manage the nuts and bolts but can't write, have no imagination and no contacts.

2. Ask for proof of the effectiveness of the campaign. PR agencies have worked so long and so hard to convince a properly sceptical public of their ability to provide measurable results that they can't deny you this request. Whether you allow yourself to be persuaded is up to you.

3. Get them to define and target each of the audiences you're interested in. If you want to communicate

with the managers of major pension funds, daily column inches in the *Sun* won't do you much good.

4. Make sure they take every opportunity to get someone else to fund your PR: a Building Society for that campaign on home security; a major brewer to promote your new book on Alehouses of the World. And so on.

9. Call in Consultancies

There are consultancies to deal with most problems and marketing is no exception. Marketing consultancies come in many shapes and sizes.

The Ad Agency as Consultancy

Advertising agencies are increasingly laying claim to marketing expertise – as a bolt on to their more profitable services. Keep in mind that there are two problems with such expertise.

1. The commission structure of advertising agencies does not sit well with the largely fee-based consultancy approach. To match usual levels of profitability within the agency they have to charge high fees relative to the service they can provide. Alternatively they are used to bring in advertising business – see 2.

2. Advertising agencies have only one solution to most business problems: advertising. This is often neither appropriate nor financially feasible.

The Big Boys

Large Management Consultancies such as Boston
Consulting Group, Bain & Co. and McKinsey's will
undoubtedly undertake marketing problems. Apart
from the clout that any recommendations will carry,
there are three things to note:

1. You may get the full rigour solution involving
   complete financial and organisational restructuring.

2. International consultancies tend to relocate their
   employees at the drop of a hat. You may never see
   the same principal twice.

3. The work is usually done by extremely bright
   young graduates with no experience of the real
   world, your world. It depends whether you like
   bright young graduates.

It goes without saying that these operations are
expensive beyond the dreams of avarice.

The Rest

A ragbag of companies and individuals. You should
expect service beyond the call of duty, creativity under
fire, an ability to meet deadlines (whatever happens),
and a certain capacity to think intelligently. Many
people believe that the last is the least important.

You have to rely on past experience and contacts
and on personal recommendations from those who
wish you well. Beware both those with too few clients
and those with too many. Remember that, as with
Market Research agencies, you are buying the skills
of one or more individuals. Make sure that they actually do your work and keep your antennae tuned for
fellow bluffers.

JARGON

Jargon is the lifeblood of the marketeer and a little will take you a long way. This, of course, is in the best tradition of marketing.

Ambient advertising – Sticking your brand in all sorts of unusual locations, e.g. pub toilets, supermarket trolleys, on the sides of cows.

Above the line – What marketeers are persuaded to spend by their advertising agency.

Below the line – What people other than advertising agencies persuade you to spend on your brands.

Brand equity – Pompous description of the state and value of your brand properties.

Brand stretching or **extension** – Fashionable tendency to 'sweat' assets. Usually ends in tears.

Bundling – Obscure Scandinavian custom of wrapping up hot-blooded adolescents of opposite sex in blankets around and between them to excite desire whilst hindering performance. Marketeers do the same thing – put two products together to persuade the gullible public they're getting a better deal.

Cannibalisation – Getting sales on one product by taking them from another of your own brands, rather than one of the competition's.

Core competences – What you are good at. The strategist's version of little white lies.

CRM – Customer Relationship Marketing (the ultimate marketing TLA (three letter acronym), the art of not sending letters out that start 'Dear Mr. Deceased'. See also:

Cause Related Marketing – Exploiting demonstrably good causes (e.g. computers in schools) for commercial ends.

Culture – How things are done in a company. Often used as a reason why something can't be done, as in "It goes against the grain of the culture here".

Cutting edge – A good thing to have in a marketing plan. Strategic planners use Differential Advantage.

Demarketing – What marketeers often do by accident, occasionally by intent: take action that decreases, rather than increases, their sales.

Diversification – The most effective commercial way of boosting egos and losing shareholders' money.

Economies of scale – Justification for grand plans.

ECR: Efficient Consumer Response – Fancy action plan.

FMCG – Fast moving consumer goods, e.g. confectionery, toiletries, groceries. **FMPG** is a variant. P stands for 'packaged'.

Four Ps – The four essentials of the marketing mix: product, price, place and promotion. You can't ignore them so don't bother to try.

Gap analysis – What you have to do to spot the gaps in the market.

Glocal Marketing – As in Think Global, Act Local.

GMO – Genetically Modified Organism. Otherwise known as killer tomatoes or Frankenfood.

Grey Panthers – The new golden oldies.

Grow, harvest, exit – The only business strategies you need: growth is good for headlines in the marketing press and getting the next job; exit is good for headlines; harvest is good for funding growth.

Inertia selling – Process by which business book clubs make more money out of you than you do out of them.

Insight – High value nuggets of consumer knowledge. Always decry boring research as "lacking insight".

KVI – Known Value Item. Change the price with care and at your peril.

LACs – Liquid Abrasive Cleaners.

Lifestyle – What the agency has and you would like.

Line extension – The knee-jerk response to NPD assignments. Just beware of adding so many variants to your existing brand that you destroy the image and cannibalise your own sales.

Marketing mixes – What results when brand managers put all the marketing ingredients together and give them a good shaking. The best mixes look good (at least on paper), taste nice, cost a lot and do a lot of damage. The acid test is who gets damaged, you or the competition?

Margin – Remember that a) all great brands have margin (it's the marketeer's bread and wine); and b) there are lots of different types of margin. Ask "Is that cash margin, or retailer margin?"

Matrix – The lego brick of marketing thinking. Do not confuse with Dot Matrix, whoever she is.

Parameter – The limit, as in "Our budget parameters don't go that far".

Projective techniques – The researcher's prerogative. Silly answers to silly questions at silly prices.

QFF – Quick Frozen Foods, e.g: burgers, peas, chips.

Scenario – The non-controversial way of breaking bad news to the Managing Director, as in "The current scenario calls for a high degree of risk management".

Share of voice – Percentage of your advertising spend relative to your competitors. The subtle question is: what share of mind is your advertising achieving?

Side of Plate – Condiments and sauces.

SKUs – Stock Keeping Units (products on supermarket shelves).

'Stealing with Pride' – Justification for nicking somebody else's idea.

SWOT – Strengths, weaknesses, opportunities, threats analysis in market planning. A.k.a. sweat analysis.

Synergy – The excuse for a number of grandiose management follies.

Test marketing – Prohibitively expensive and very public way of demonstrating how well you've organised a new product launch.

The Three Rs – The Product Manager's Life-Cycle: Repackage, Relaunch and Resign.

Viral Marketing – Getting consumers to act as salesmen for your products; in the old economy known as 'word of mouth'.

White spaces – Gaps in the portfolio which can be creatively filled in brainstorming sessions.

Windscreen wiper brand management – First one idea, then another...

THE AUTHORS

Graham Harding started life in rural Essex before grabbing a few glittering prizes in Cambridge. His inability to read medieval Latin and a vague desire to do something useful ended thoughts of academic life. He therefore launched himself on the jobs market as a publisher and spent several happy years learning about the less sophisticated side of marketing.

Repositioning as a fully fledged marketing man was the logical next step. A period of line extension and a desire for higher penetration took him to The Value Engineers, a successful and highly individual Marketing Consultancy.

This guide is his first venture into print under his own name. The others were much more prestigious but he is not at liberty to reveal them. His ambition is to write a book that will make real money.

Paul Walton was conceived in Walsall, test marketed at Brasenose College, Oxford, and launched at a Paddington advertising agency.

His first products included Swedish cars, German lager and British Intelligence. Assigned to a food account he early distinguished himself in new product development by recommending that the clients' starch-reduced rolls should be relaunched as loft insulation materials.

After 10 years of developing products for other people, and a major awayday with himself, he finally launched his own product: The Value Engineers. A keen student of history, his *Mastermind* specialist subject would be; 'The Cooking Sauce Market – 1974 to the present day'.

www.bluffers.com

for other titles in the Bluffer's Guide® series